COMPOSER SHOWCASE
HAL LEONARD STUDENT PIANO LIBRARY

LATE INTERMEDIATE LEVEL

Garden Treasures

VE PIECES FOR PIANO SOLO

BY CAROL KLOSE

T0080101

CONTENTS

ISBN 978-1-4234-8320-5

HAL•LEONARD®
CORPORATION

7777 W. BLUEMOUND RD. P.O. BOX 13819 MILWAUKEE, WI 53213

In Australia Contact:
Hal Leonard Australia Pty. Ltd.
4 Lentara Court
Cheltenham, Victoria, 3192 Australia
Email: ausadmin@halleonard.com.au

Visit Hal Leonard Online at
www.halleonard.com

The kiss of the sun for pardon,
The song of the birds for mirth.
One is nearer God's heart in a garden
Than anywhere else on earth.

—Dorothy Frances Gurney, "Garden Thoughts"

Dedication

I have always admired gardeners, plant lovers with a 'green thumb' – people whose passion is to plant, hoe, weed, water and feed, and who know their *pelargonium* from their *Eustoma grandiflorum*. My husband, mother, three sisters, and numerous friends all belong to this special group who make it possible for the rest of us to bask in the beauty of a "garden."

The pieces in *Garden Treasures* are dedicated to these and all gardeners, including the gifted British garden and landscape designer, Jinny Blom, who was such an inspiration for the music (see Performance Notes for "Water Lily Garden"). The beauty that results from their devotion to a simple patch of land is a source of boundless inspiration, joy, and love for anyone who has stooped to smell a rose.

I especially want to thank my husband John for sharing with me the loving gift of his garden season after season…

—Carol Klose

Performance Notes

Water Lily Garden

There is a special reason that this piece is dedicated to Jinny Blom – English master gardener, landscape designer and winner of the Gold Award at the 2007 Chelsea Flower Show. Upon hearing Jinny lecture in Illinois recently, I was inspired by the way she spoke of her designs as unfolding creations, much as a composer would talk about his own music. I was so struck by the beauty of her gardens as shown in her slide presentation that I could hardly wait to get home and start composing "Water Lily Garden."

The image in this music is of a garden that features a small quiet pond dotted with elegant white water lilies. The *poco più mosso* section beginning at measure 25 is reminiscent of French Impressionistic "water" music. The return to the opening theme in measure 37 is dappled with unusual harmonies that end mysteriously as if with an unresolved question.

- In the opening A section, bring out the RH melody line with expressive tone. Keep the eighth-note accompaniment patterns very light. Use the *ritards* as a guide for *rubato*.
- At measure 19, the music becomes more carefree, with the hands shifting between various positions on the keys. End each slur with a slight wrist lift to propel the hand to each new position gracefully.
- At measure 25, imagine water droplets, perhaps in a nearby fountain. Pass the notes gracefully from hand to hand with gentle slurs, avoiding unwanted accents.
- After the whole-tone scale and motives in the transition in measures 33-36, be sure to blend the end of measure 36 into the next section with an unhurried *ritard* that carries into the slower tempo of the opening.
- With an even slower tempo and una corda pedal at measure 46, let the piece mysteriously die out to nothing *(morendo)* at the end.

Dandelion Wishes

Remember how much fun it is to pick dandelions with fluffy seeds and blow them so the seeds take flight in the breeze? I like to wish with each puff, hoping my wishes will come true as I watch the seeds scatter out of sight.

The arpeggios between the hands in the A and A1 sections in this piece are like fluffy dandelion seeds drifting gracefully in the breeze. The spirit of the B section is more thoughtful, like a nocturne, perhaps dreaming of the wish. The grace-note *gruppetto* scale in the final measure finds the seeds disappearing with a gentle whisp of air.

- In the A and A1 sections, use a graceful *legato* touch when passing the notes from one hand to the other. End each slur gracefully, with a slight lift of the wrist.
- Play the LH *tenuto* notes with more weight behind the hand. Listen for the resulting counter-melody as the *tenuto* notes support the surrounding broken-chord and melodic patterns.
- Shape ascending and descending eighth-note patterns with a *crescendo* and *decrescendo.*
- In the B section (meas. 21-42), focus on a warm tone for the RH *cantabile* melody, and use a light touch for the LH notes on beats 2, 3, and 4.
- The final grace-note *gruppetto* is merely a D major scale: a LH tetrachord quickly followed by one in the RH. Practice playing these notes as lightly, seamlessly and quickly as possible. Imagine blowing the fluffy dandelion seeds into the air. Take time to pause for an instant before "blowing" to make a wish!

The Healing Garden

In times of trial I find great peace in a quiet garden – whether sitting among the flowers at home, walking in the splendid local botanical gardens, or recalling treasured memories of lovely cottage gardens in our travels through the English countryside.

I composed this hymn-like piece with the following words in mind: "Where peace abides is where I would be." The first notes of the theme (m. 5-8) seem to fit those lyrics. The piece begins as a chorale in C major, gradually growing in texture, and finally modulating to E-flat major in measure 29, where the theme returns with powerful pianistic fullness created by arpeggiated patterns in both hands. The quiet ending seems to confirm the healing spirit of this special musical garden.

- Be sure to breathe each phrase as if singing. In meas. 5-8, think or sing the words, "Where peace abides is where I would be." You may make up your own words for the rest of the phrases if you wish. Observe the *ritards* for a built-in *rubato*.
- Listen for RH balance as you bring out the top notes in measures 5-28. Practice playing the RH melody notes only, then add the harmony notes more softly.
- In the first half of the piece, phrases often end with sus (suspension) chords and resolutions typical of chorale style (ex. measure 8, 12, 16, 20). Lean into the dissonant note, and play its resolution note(s) with a *decrescendo*.
- Beginning at measure 30, the theme returns in the key of E-flat major with arpeggio patterns in both hands. Play this section with a full, warm "concerto" sound. The RH melody notes are marked *tenuto*. To hear the harmonic skeleton, first find and play each RH *tenuto* note and add the single LH note that accompanies it. Then gradually fill in the other broken-chord tones, increasing the speed as you become more comfortable. Be sure to observe the fingering carefully.

Jasmine in the Mist

While working on my graduate degree in Italy, I had the privilege of living and studying for two years in a 16-century villa outside Florence. This piece was inspired by memories of exotic jasmine vines growing on the centuries-old walls of that villa nestled in the Tuscan hills. At night, the heavy perfume of jasmine permeated the warm air, while in the misty Tuscan rain the white flowers took on a dreamy, surreal appearance.

The piece begins with a gentle RH motive whose rhythm in 3/4 time becomes the basis for the themes in the rest of the piece. The opening misty atmosphere grows into a gentle rain by measure 33. At the B section beginning in measure 51, the feel of a swaying waltz takes over as the jasmine vines bend gently to and fro in the drizzly breeze. At measure 67 the returning A theme becomes strong and dramatic, almost concerto-like, gradually tapering off as the rain turns to mist, then disappearing with the *ppp* arpeggiated chord in the final measures.

- In the opening measures, play the LH eighth notes like a soft swoosh of air. Use the *una corda* pedal and a very light touch through measure 32.
- The F diminished chord in measures 11 and 12 returns in measure 84. In each case practice the LH alone first; then add each RH two-note slur, leaning into the first note and playing the second note with a *diminuendo*.
- Do not be tempted to release the damper pedal during measures 13-32. The sounds should mingle together as if almost "invisible" in the foggy mist.
- Whenever the melody is played by the LH, use a very light touch for the accompanying RH broken chords and octaves.
- In measures 51-62, play the RH melody with more weight behind the hand for tone. Feel those valse-like measures in "one."
- Play the delicate final arpeggiated chord very quickly and quietly.

Daffodil Caprice

I wandered lonely as a cloud
That floats on high o'er vales and hills,
When all at once I saw a crowd,
A host, of golden daffodils;
Beside the lake, beneath the trees,
Fluttering and dancing in the breeze
Continuous as the stars that shine
And twinkle on the milky way,
They stretched in never-ending line
Along the margin of a bay:
Ten thousand saw I at a glance,
Tossing their heads in sprightly dance.

—William Wordsworth, "I Wandered Lonely as a Cloud," 1804

Daffodils are such cheerful signs of Spring! In this piece, I imagine a garden full of the bright yellow blossoms tossing their sunny little heads in defiance of the last cruel winds of winter's grip. The non-stop momentum in the piece should reflect straight-ahead joy and exuberance interspersed with moments of scherzo-like playful attitude changes. Within the Coda (measures 70-73), perhaps a final shiver of cold air slowly makes its way across the garden. The single bird "tweet" in measure 72 seems to ask, "Are you SURE Spring is really here?" However, the return to the original bright tempo and joyful spirit in the ending leaves no doubt!

- To learn the piece quickly, look for patterns repeated in various combinations and on various pitches throughout the piece.
- Study the transpositions of the RH "add 2" chords (ex. m. 21, beat 1) and accompanying LH patterns for quick memorization.
- Keep the rhythmic momentum going without pause until measure 70. Feel each 4/4 measure in "two," and each 3/4 measure in "one."
- Play the pedaled motives warmly with romantic flair, without slowing the pulse.
- For the crossover LH chords, hold the chord formation in the LH and stay close to the keys through the crisp staccatos.

Water Lily Garden

for Jinny Blom

by Carol Klose

Plaintively, with expression (♩ = c. 108)

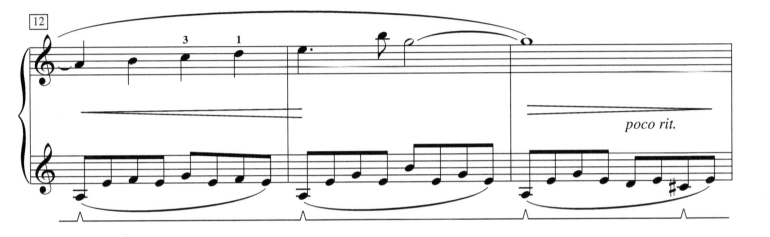

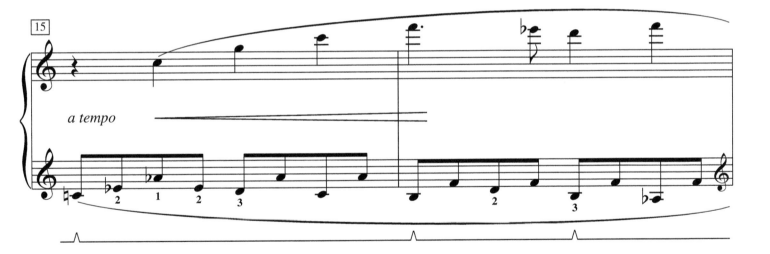

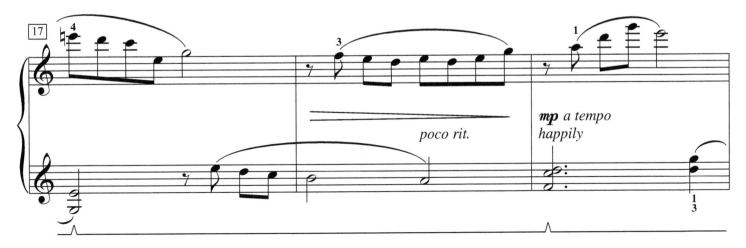

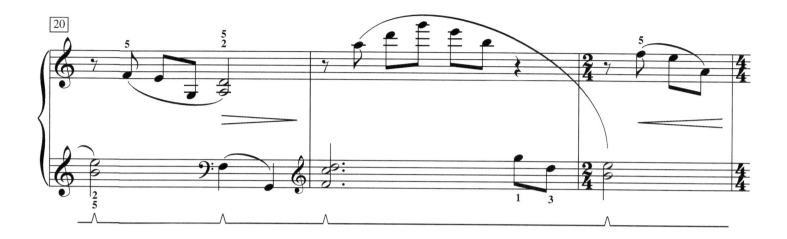

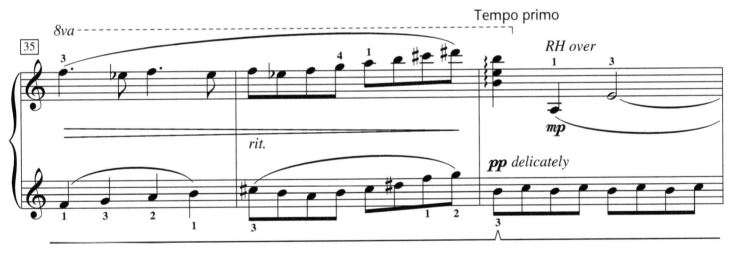

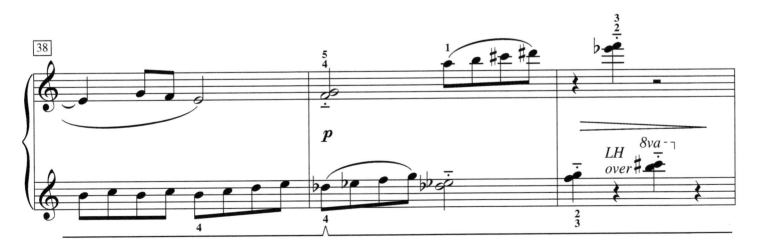

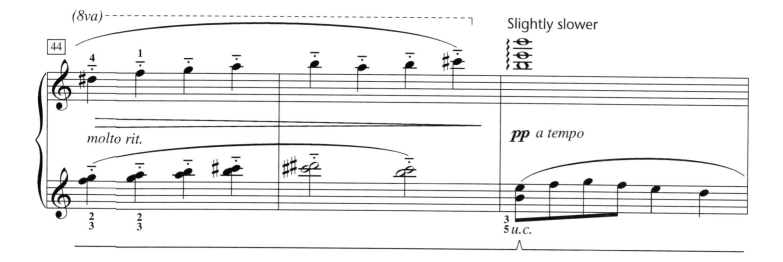

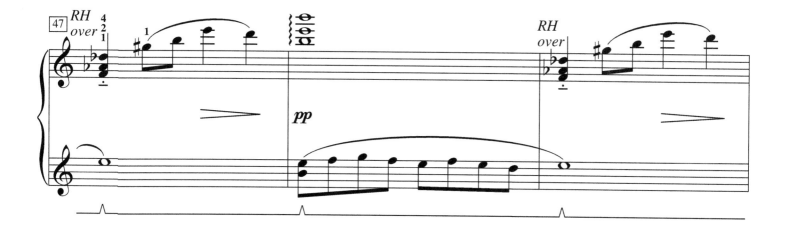

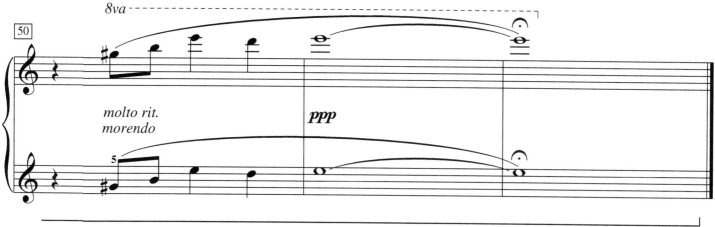

(1'52")

Dandelion Wishes

By Carol Klose

Andante con moto ($\,\rule[0.4ex]{0.8em}{0.1ex}$ = c. 60)

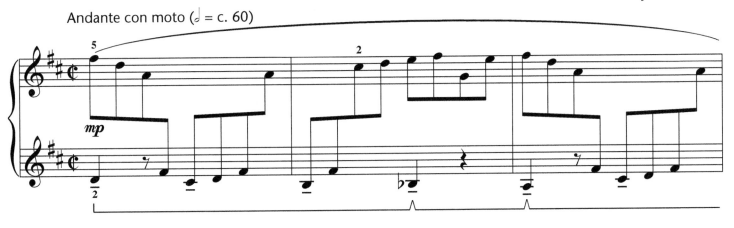

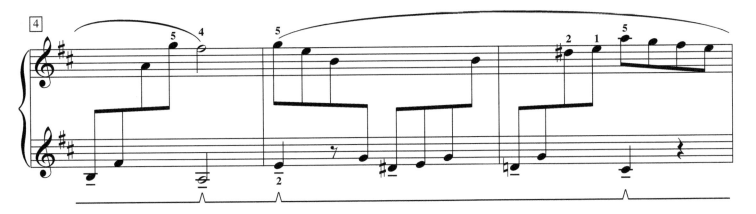

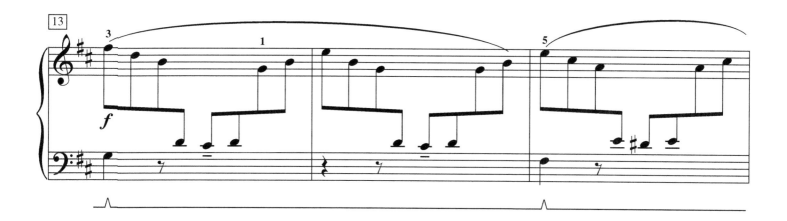

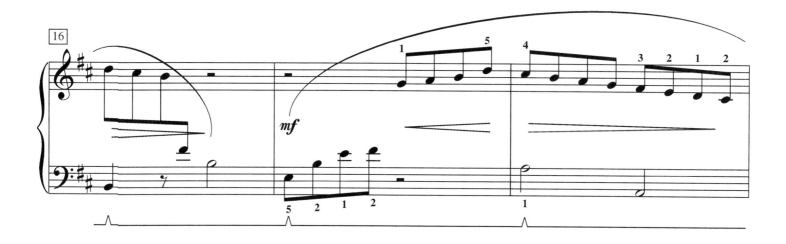

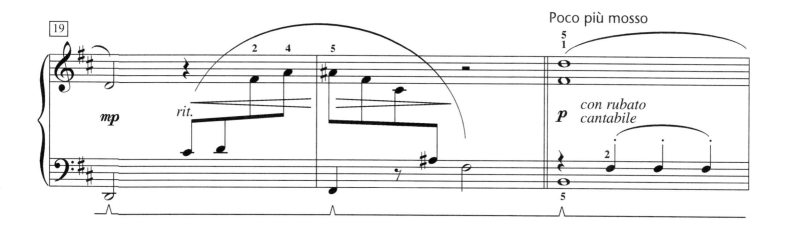

Poco più mosso

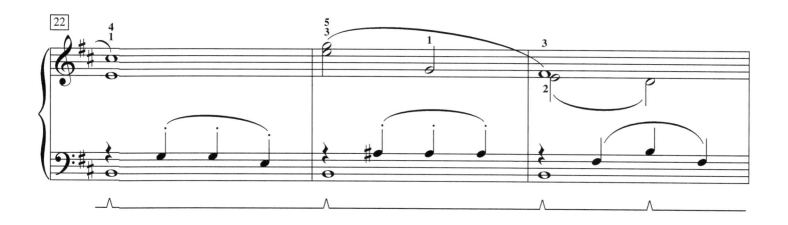

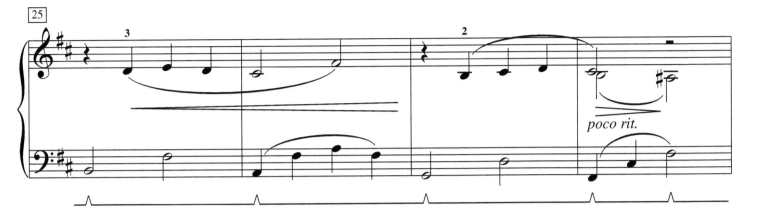

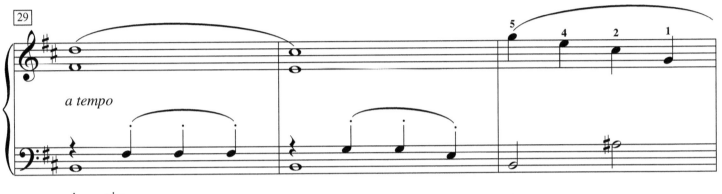

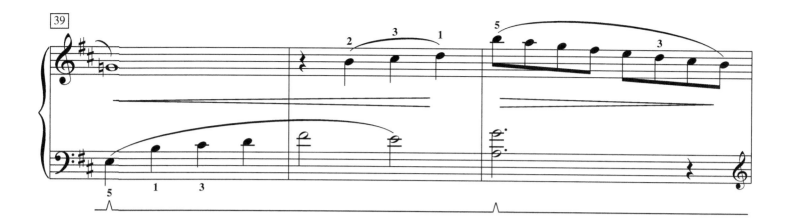

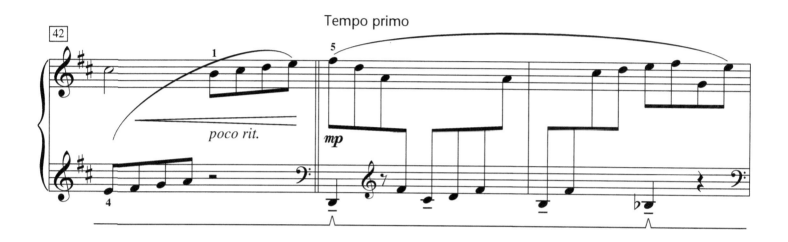

Tempo primo

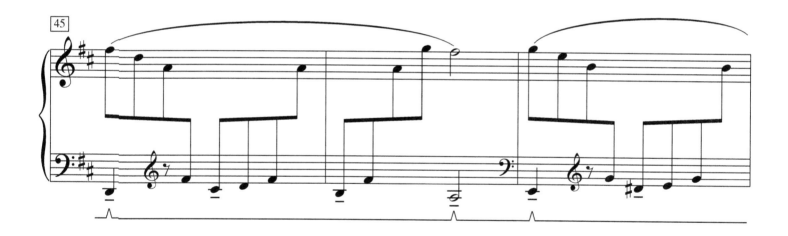

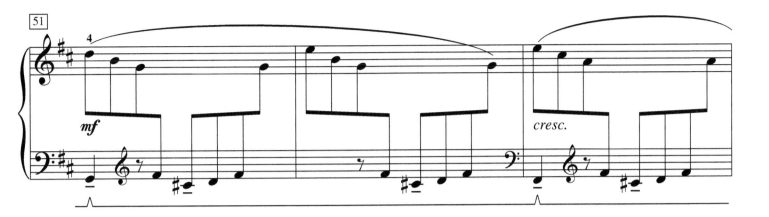

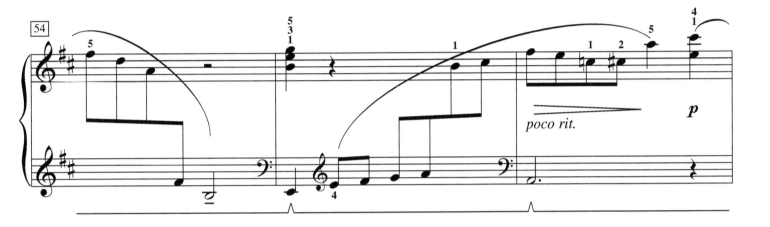

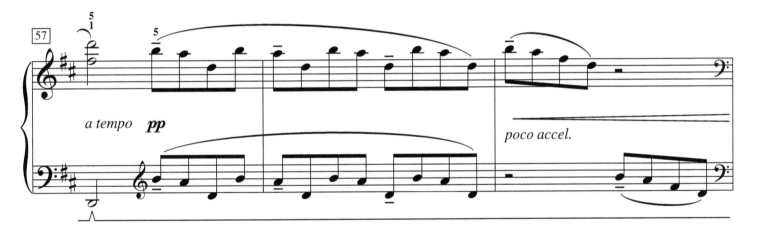

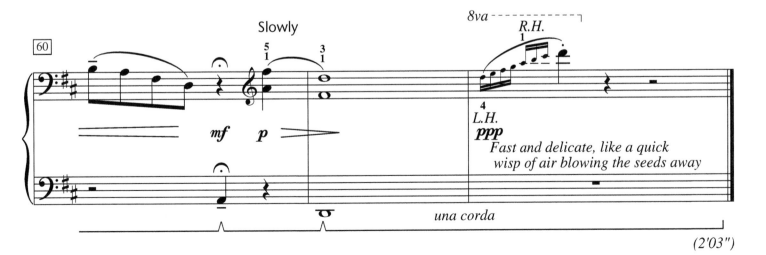

The Healing Garden

By Carol Klose

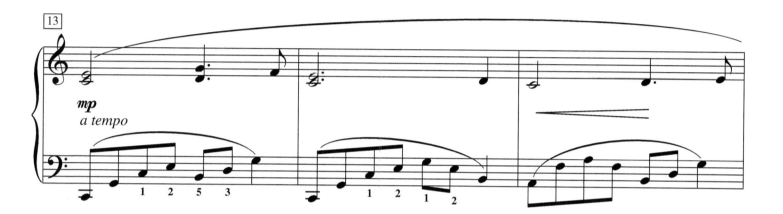

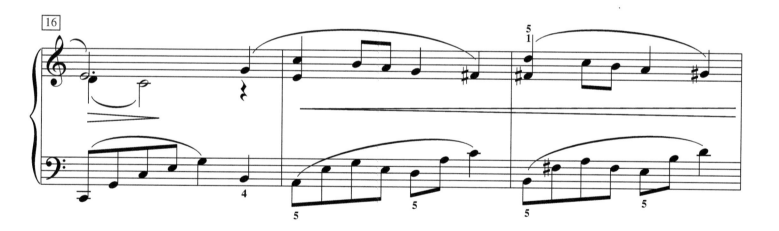

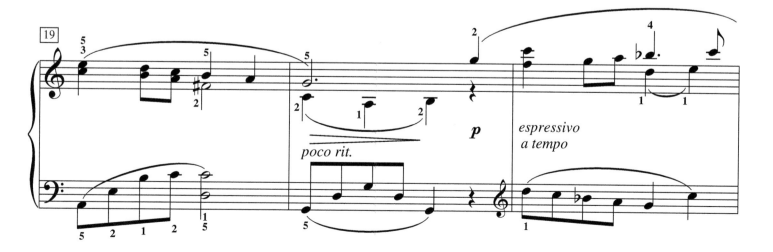

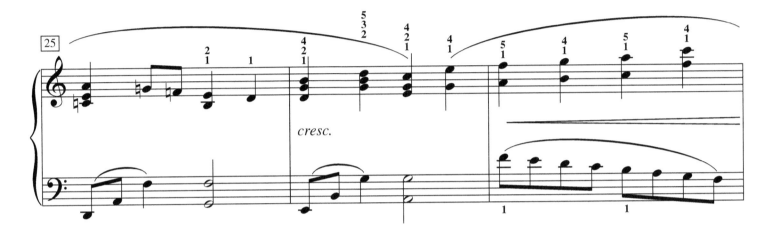

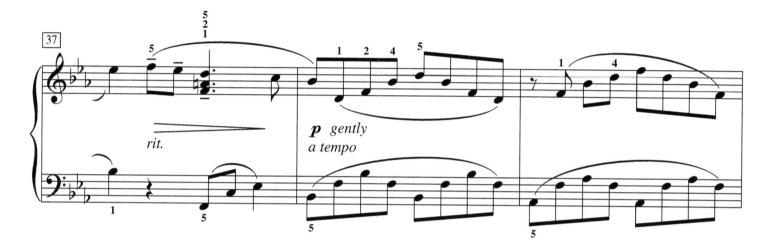

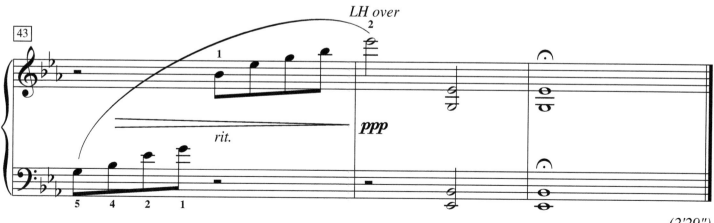

(2'29")

Jasmine in the Mist

for my husband John

By Carol Klose

Moderato (♩=112)

Like misty raindrops (♩ = 120)

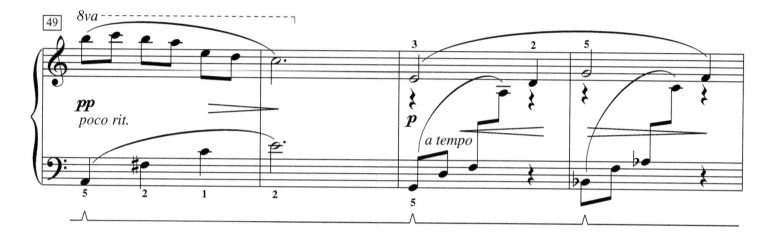

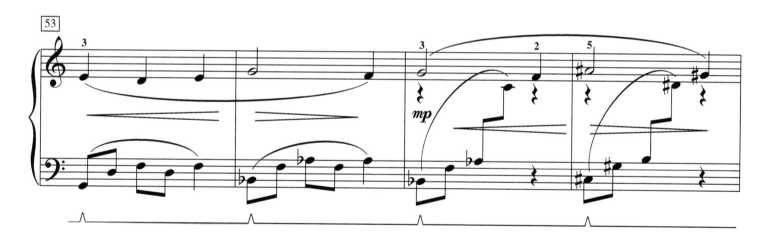

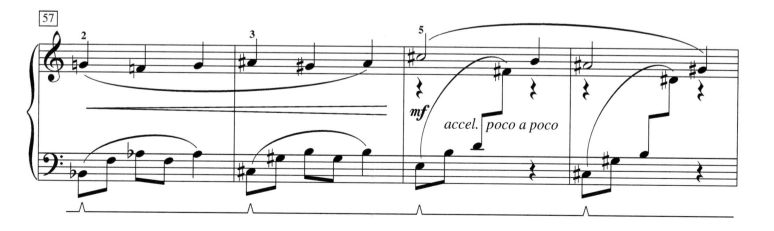

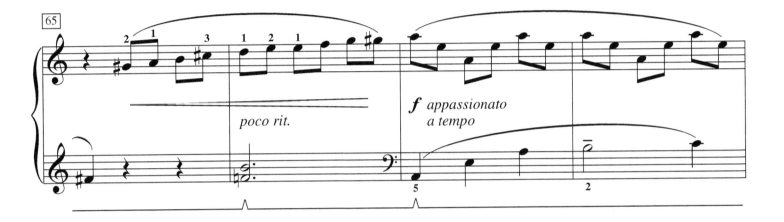

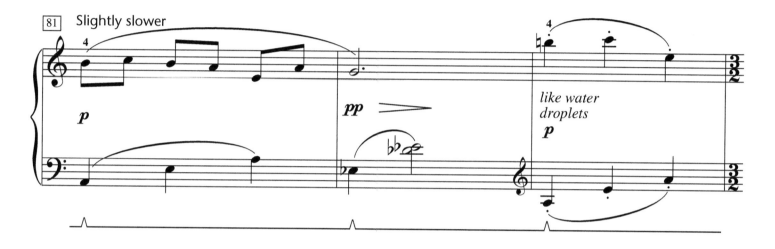

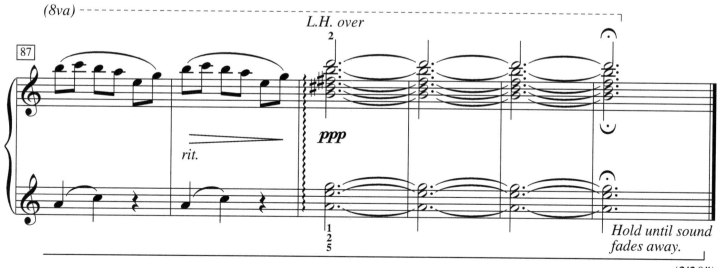

Daffodil Caprice

By Carol Klose

Brightly (♩ = 184-200)

mf scherzando

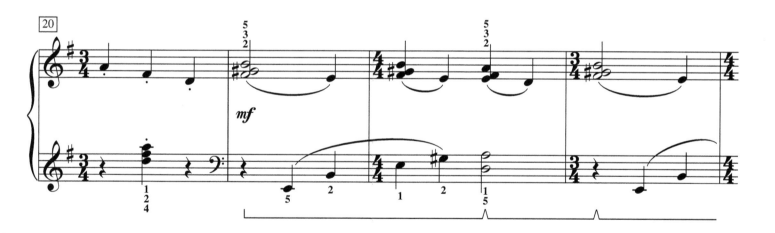

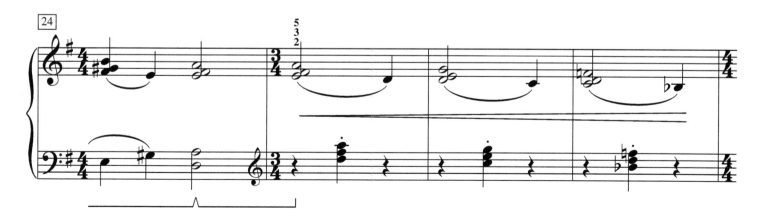

L.H. over R.H.

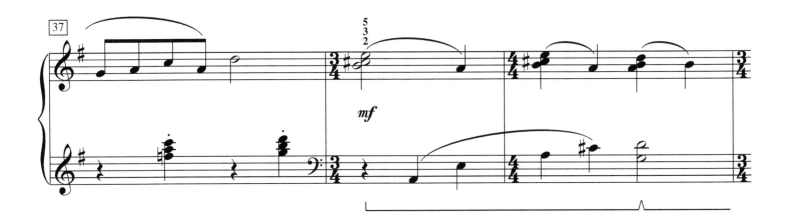

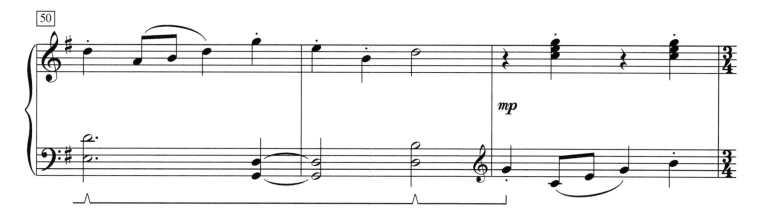

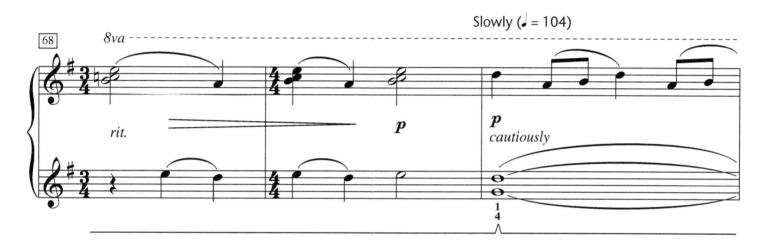

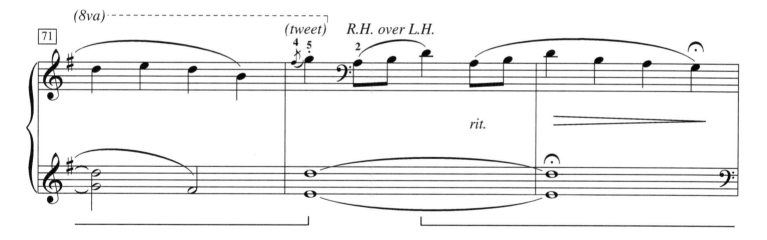

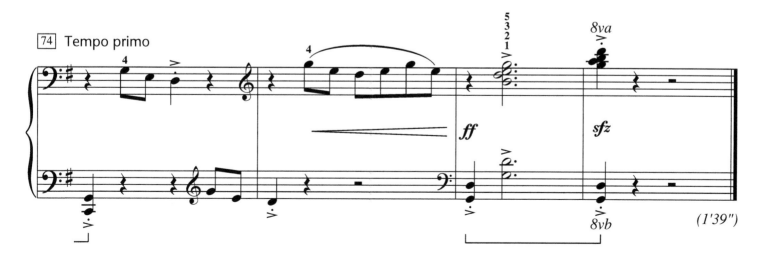

COMPOSER SHOWCASE
HAL LEONARD STUDENT PIANO LIBRARY

This series showcases great original piano music from our **Hal Leonard Student Piano Library** family of composers. Carefully graded for easy selection.

BILL BOYD

JAZZ BITS (AND PIECES)
Early Intermediate Level
00290312 11 Solos......................$7.99

JAZZ DELIGHTS
Intermediate Level
00240435 11 Solos......................$8.99

JAZZ FEST
Intermediate Level
00240436 10 Solos......................$8.99

JAZZ PRELIMS
Early Elementary Level
00290032 12 Solos......................$7.99

JAZZ SKETCHES
Intermediate Level
00220001 8 Solos........................$8.99

JAZZ STARTERS
Elementary Level
00290425 10 Solos......................$8.99

JAZZ STARTERS II
Late Elementary Level
00290434 11 Solos......................$7.99

JAZZ STARTERS III
Late Elementary Level
00290465 12 Solos......................$8.99

THINK JAZZ!
Early Intermediate Level
00290417 Method Book............$12.99

TONY CARAMIA

JAZZ MOODS
Intermediate Level
00296728 8 Solos........................$6.95

SUITE DREAMS
Intermediate Level
00296775 4 Solos........................$6.99

SONDRA CLARK

DAKOTA DAYS
Intermediate Level
00296521 5 Solos........................$6.95

FLORIDA FANTASY SUITE
Intermediate Level
00296766 3 Duets.......................$7.95

THREE ODD METERS
Intermediate Level
00296472 3 Duets.......................$6.95

MATTHEW EDWARDS

**CONCERTO FOR
YOUNG PIANISTS**
FOR 2 PIANOS, FOUR HANDS
Intermediate Level Book/CD
00296356 3 Movements $19.99

CONCERTO NO. 2 IN G MAJOR
FOR 2 PIANOS, 4 HANDS
Intermediate Level Book/CD
00296670 3 Movements............$17.99

PHILLIP KEVEREN

MOUSE ON A MIRROR
Late Elementary Level
00296361 5 Solos........................$8.99

MUSICAL MOODS
Elementary/Late Elementary Level
00296714 7 Solos........................$6.99

SHIFTY-EYED BLUES
Late Elementary Level
00296374 5 Solos........................$7.99

CAROL KLOSE

THE BEST OF CAROL KLOSE
Early to Late Intermediate Level
00146151 15 Solos....................$12.99

CORAL REEF SUITE
Late Elementary Level
00296354 7 Solos........................$7.50

DESERT SUITE
Intermediate Level
00296667 6 Solos........................$7.99

FANCIFUL WALTZES
Early Intermediate Level
00296473 5 Solos........................$7.95

GARDEN TREASURES
Late Intermediate Level
00296787 5 Solos........................$8.50

ROMANTIC EXPRESSIONS
Intermediate to Late Intermediate Level
00296923 5 Solos........................$8.99

WATERCOLOR MINIATURES
Early Intermediate Level
00296848 7 Solos........................$7.99

JENNIFER LINN

AMERICAN IMPRESSIONS
Intermediate Level
00296471 6 Solos........................$8.99

ANIMALS HAVE FEELINGS TOO
Early Elementary/Elementary Level
00147789 8 Solos........................$8.99

AU CHOCOLAT
Late Elementary/Early Intermediate Level
00298110 7 Solos........................$8.99

CHRISTMAS IMPRESSIONS
Intermediate Level
00296706 8 Solos........................$8.99

JUST PINK
Elementary Level
00296722 9 Solos........................$8.99

LES PETITES IMAGES
Late Elementary Level
00296664 7 Solos........................$8.99

LES PETITES IMPRESSIONS
Intermediate Level
00296355 6 Solos........................$8.99

REFLECTIONS
Late Intermediate Level
00296843 5 Solos........................$8.99

TALES OF MYSTERY
Intermediate Level
00296769 6 Solos........................$8.99

LYNDA LYBECK-ROBINSON

ALASKA SKETCHES
Early Intermediate Level
00119637 8 Solos........................$8.99

AN AWESOME ADVENTURE
Late Elementary Level
00137563 8 Solos........................$7.99

FOR THE BIRDS
Early Intermediate/Intermediate Level
00237078 9 Solos........................$8.99

WHISPERING WOODS
Late Elementary Level
00275905 9 Solos........................$8.99

MONA REJINO

CIRCUS SUITE
Late Elementary Level
00296665 5 Solos........................$8.99

COLOR WHEEL
Early Intermediate Level
00201951 6 Solos........................$9.99

IMPRESIONES DE ESPAÑA
Intermediate Level
00337520 6 Solos........................$8.99

IMPRESSIONS OF NEW YORK
Intermediate Level
00364212......................................$8.99

JUST FOR KIDS
Elementary Level
00296840 8 Solos........................$7.99

MERRY CHRISTMAS MEDLEYS
Intermediate Level
00296799 5 Solos........................$8.99

MINIATURES IN STYLE
Intermediate Level
00148088 6 Solos........................$8.99

PORTRAITS IN STYLE
Early Intermediate Level
00296507 6 Solos........................$8.99

EUGÉNIE ROCHEROLLE

CELEBRATION SUITE
Intermediate Level
00152724 3 Duets.......................$8.99

**ENCANTOS ESPAÑOLES
(SPANISH DELIGHTS)**
Intermediate Level
00125451 6 Solos........................$8.99

JAMBALAYA
Intermediate Level
00296654 2 Pianos, 8 Hands.....$12.99
00296725 2 Pianos, 4 Hands........$7.95

JEROME KERN CLASSICS
Intermediate Level
00296577 10 Solos....................$12.99

LITTLE BLUES CONCERTO
Early Intermediate Level
00142801 2 Pianos, 4 Hands......$12.99

TOUR FOR TWO
Late Elementary Level
00296832 6 Duets.......................$9.99

TREASURES
Late Elementary/Early Intermediate Level
00296924 7 Solos........................$8.99

JEREMY SISKIND

BIG APPLE JAZZ
Intermediate Level
00278209 8 Solos........................$8.99

MYTHS AND MONSTERS
Late Elementary/Early Intermediate Level
00148148 9 Solos........................$8.99

CHRISTOS TSITSAROS

**DANCES FROM AROUND
THE WORLD**
Early Intermediate Level
00296688 7 Solos........................$8.99

FIVE SUMMER PIECES
Late Intermediate/Advanced Level
00361235 5 Solos......................$12.99

LYRIC BALLADS
Intermediate/Late Intermediate Level
00102404 6 Solos........................$8.99

POETIC MOMENTS
Intermediate Level
00296403 8 Solos........................$8.99

SEA DIARY
Early Intermediate Level
00253486 9 Solos........................$8.99

SONATINA HUMORESQUE
Late Intermediate Level
00296772 3 Movements............$6.99

SONGS WITHOUT WORDS
Intermediate Level
00296506 9 Solos........................$9.99

THREE PRELUDES
Early Advanced Level
00130747 3 Solos........................$8.99

THROUGHOUT THE YEAR
Late Elementary Level
00296723 12 Duets.....................$6.95

ADDITIONAL COLLECTIONS

AT THE LAKE
by Elvina Pearce
Elementary/Late Elementary Level
00131642 10 Solos and Duets.....$7.99

CHRISTMAS FOR TWO
by Dan Fox
Early Intermediate Level
00290069 13 Duets....................$8.99

CHRISTMAS JAZZ
by Mike Springer
Intermediate Level
00296525 6 Solos........................$8.99

COUNTY RAGTIME FESTIVAL
by Fred Kern
Intermediate Level
00296882 7 Solos........................$7.99

LITTLE JAZZERS
by Jennifer Watts
Elementary/Late Elementary Level
00154573 9 Solos........................$8.99

PLAY THE BLUES!
by Luann Carman
Early Intermediate Level
00296357 10 Solos....................$9.99

ROLLER COASTERS & RIDES
by Jennifer & Mike Watts
Intermediate Level
00131144 8 Duets.......................$8.99

HAL•LEONARD®
www.halleonard.com